Reverberations of
the Genome

poems by James Grabill

Acknowledgements – Reverberations of the Genome

The author gratefully acknowledges publications in which these poems and prose poems originally appeared (at times in other form):

Arabesques (Algeria): "Nuclear Sun"

The Bitter Oleander (US): "The Brain and Animals"

The Blue Mountain Review (US): "Song"

Caliban Online (US): "Reading the Air" & "Through the Door to Where They Were"

Chariton Review (US): "Lunch Fractals"

Cold Mountain Review (US): "Return the Bees to Plants on the Planet"

The Decadent Review (US): "Reverberation of the Genome" & "So Light Plants Its Root"

Deluge (US): "In the Wilds"

Elohi Gadugi (US): "Night Songs and Sleep"

Gargoyle (US): "Out of Unfathomable Time"

Granite (US): "Distant Weather," "Divisions," & "Tongues"

Hamilton Stone Review (US): "Grasshopper Clouds" & "Seated at the Table"

Heliotrope (US): "Avenue of Falling Rain"

kayak (US): "Song from Before"

The Kerf (US): "Bay of Light" & "Being Continues to Begin"

Laurel Review (US): "Night Crickets"

Miramar (US): "Salt on the Table"

Panache (US): "The Edge"

Phantom Drift (US): "A Few Steps Out the Door"

Poet Lore (US): "Summer Hieroglyphics"

Poetry Northwest (US): "Memory of the Birds," "Memory of the Carnival," "The Next Key," & "Trees"

Seisma (US): "The Size of a Person on Earth"

South Dakota Review (US): "Inside the Blood, Rain Is Falling"
Stand (UK): "Breaking Out of the Pen" & "Risk of Yes or No"
Terrain: A Journal of the Built and Natural Environments (US):
     "Wind's Always on the Road" & "With Heat Going Up"
Unlikely Stories (US): "Written on Dream Skins"
Weber— The Contemporary West (US): "I'll See You at the Concert
     of Doves," "It Isn't Known, Until It Is," & "What Is More"
Wilderness House Literary Review (US): "Birdwatching"
Windfall (US): "Before Summer"

I'd like to express gratitude to L. Bernstein, W. Marsalis, R. Shankar, & A. A. Khan; to V. Van Gogh, W. Kandinsky, M. Rothko, & M. Chagall; to B. Dylan, N. Young, J. Mitchell, & Lennon & McCartney; to G. Kinnell, G. Snyder, R. Bly, & P. Neruda; to W. Whitman. R.W. Emerson, & T.S. Eliot; to D. Raphael, B. Tremblay, C. Howell, D. Sheffield, H. McCord, J. Tipton, & B. Witherup; to P. Petersen, D. Averill, V. Orr, & B. Siverly; to J. Bradley, R. Gonzalez, G. Kalamaras, P. Woods, L. & J. Zimmerman, & Leon; to J. Kaady, J. Sherard, W. Carlile, & M. Nelson. And most of all to M. Burki — for unending encouragement, engagement, and love of the arts & other species.

Music can name the unnamable and communicate
the unknowable. — **Leonard Bernstein**

Those who dwell among the beauties and mysteries of the earth are
never alone or weary of life. Those who contemplate the beauty of
the earth find reserves of strength that will endure as long as life
lasts. The more clearly we can focus our attention on the wonders
and realities of the universe, the less taste we shall have for destruction.

— **Rachel Carson**

Seed is not just the source of life. It is the very foundation of our being.

— **Vandana Shiva**

To work on behalf of the wild is to restore culture.

— **Gary Snyder**

Contents – Reverberations of the Genome

I.

REVERBERATION OF THE GENOME 10
    I. The Symbiosis in Diego Rivera 10
    II. As the Sun Soars Over 12
    III. In Schoenberg Mind 13
    IV. Blue Fin in the Seas of Hemingway 14
BEFORE SUMMER 16
BAY OF LIGHT 17
READING THE AIR 18
BEING CONTINUES TO BEGIN 19
THROUGH THE DOOR TO WHERE THEY WERE 20
AVENUE OF FALLING RAIN 23
YELLOW CANDLE 25
HALF PATH 27
LUNCH FRACTALS 28
SONGS FROM FAR BACK 31
    I. Sunday 31
    II. The Next Key 31
    III. Tongues 31
    IV. Divisions 32
    V. Song from Before 32
    VI. Memory of the Birds 33
    VII. The Flutes 33
    VIII. Distant Weather 33
    IX. Memory of the Carnival 34
    X. The Edge 35
    XI. Trees 35
    XII. Harbor 35
APPLE 36
I'LL SEE YOU AT THE CONCERT OF DOVES 37

II.

SEATED AT THE TABLE 40
THE BRAIN AND ANIMALS 41
GRASSHOPPER CLOUDS 43
YARD CONTROL 44
BREAKING OUT OF THE PEN 45
RISK OF YES OR NO 46
RETURN BEES TO PLANTS ON THE PLANET 47
NUCLEAR SUN 49
    I. Hieroglyphic Dust in the Air 49
    II. Walking Beneath Cottonwoods 49
    III. Afternoon Lit by Breakers 50
    IV. Morning Sun 50
WITH HEAT GOING UP 52
HAVING LESS 53
SALT ON THE TABLE 54
SUMMER HIEROGLYPHICS 57
    I. End of the Week 57
    II. Unexpected Levitation 57
    III. Tomato 58
    IV. Planets Lined Up in the West 58
    V. Dark and Light Evening 59
    VI. Bending with the Road 60
    VII. Down a Telescope's Focus 60
    VIII. Crackling Power Grid 61
IT ISN'T KNOWN UNTIL IT IS 62

III.

THE SIZE OF A PERSON ON EARTH 64
BIRDWATCHING 65
SO LIGHT PLANTS ITS ROOT 69
    I. Bearing the Beautiful Collision in Rothko 69
    II. In the Room with Paul Klee 71

III. Pollock Painting Organic Expression 72

IV. The Light in Paintings of Morris Graves 74

WRITTEN ON DREAM SKINS 75

IN THE WILDS 76

INSIDE THE BLOOD, RAIN IS FALLING 77

WIND'S ALWAYS ON THE ROAD 80

OUT OF UNFATHOMABLE TIME 82

WHAT IS MORE 83

A FEW STEPS OUT THE DOOR 85

A FEW SAYINGS UNDER THE SKY 86

NIGHT CRICKETS 88

NIGHT SONGS AND SLEEP 90

EARTH ALIVE 91

I. This Instant 91

II. In Rings of Trees 92

III. Remaking the World 93

IV. Every Feather Shows Nerve 94

V. Breath Is the Wind in Blood 95

SONG 97

I.

Innovation never happens as planned. — **Gifford Pinchot**

The truth is, natural organisms have managed to do
everything we want to do without guzzling fossil fuels,
polluting the planet or mortgaging the future.

— **Janine Benyus**

REVERBERATION OF THE GENOME

> And so the new thinking now within the scientific community
> about the way genes and environment interact is more like a
> piano with our genes as the keyboard, if you will, and the
> environment as the hands of the pianist. You could play Bach or
> you could play improvisational jazz— it's the same keyboard, it's
> the same DNA but the environmental messages have changed.
>
> - **Sandra Steingraber**

I. The Symbiosis in Diego Rivera

Out of suffering wants and calm core
of the exquisite instrument of cells,
what lives within the human resonates,
buoyant on gravity, in the rock of day
long into night that unfolds over eons,
in layers thick with final insinuations
of human shoulders and their clashes.
After pre-industrial ambition quickened,
it returned to the ground of its making
to extract raw materials and buried fuels.
It's underneath now, migrating with 2-day
clouds of passenger pigeons that shut down
the sky dark with their bodies flying over
through breath, in the firmament of air,
eating berries and worms, for seed-mind
reaching out in daylight that awakened
the cells, with solar resonance giving shape
to winds that circulate before communicating
through veins. So we've carried our weight

through blood-borne matter which the day
engenders, transporting all of it into night.
Where the mind has been an emanation
of symbiosis, competing to survive grows old,
redefining us as we speak. Microorganisms
are an ocean everywhere what we were given
stands, as present labors transport us
to the past-peopled ground floors in time.

II. As the Sun Soars Over Rodin's Towering Human Figures

Bees following their maps lightly touch
the origin and then return to hives
through the invisibility of air,
where the molecular wilds are burning
with electricity, the apparatus of beauty
in the genome wheeling open in sync
with the overhead stars, however much
of the past or future we might be forgetting,
with the route home planted within
cells of our muscles and bones.
The project of hives is to keep the genome
reaching, interconnecting destinies
of species, where egg-splitting detonations
of fossil thunders achieve critical mass,
when new generations imprint on the world
as they grow up, assuming what they see
is only natural, while childhood
communion bypasses the mind,
sinking rudimentary choruses of belief
into spots where the story concerns
what stays or must go, whether you'd like
a little more future on the plate
with your present or believe mercy cultures
ought to take care of everyone
or the sun at the center of waking
in the solar system ought to be enough
to show where we are and forgive us.

III. In Schoenberg Mind

Every second passes almost
instantly into nothing
we'll see again, though we'll recall
what happened to strike us
or connect us with more of the whole,
or what's fit into a frame developed
and harnessed by central mind
along with two-handed neon clocks
and restoration lofts for the half-classified
high-rise museum of central intelligence.
And yet each second is presence
impossible to measure without activating
large numbers of flora and fauna
with whole systems of elemental support
connected to sources of rivers
and women working the conveyor,
kids forced to crawl down into diamond
mines, chickens mulling around
the barnyard in June overflowing
with mystery where consciousness is
practicing before it performs. Each second
an ethical chance buoys up being here,
present in a working nervous system
with integrative comprehension,
a supersensory emanation of waking
and sleeping outside the frame,
while the collaborating cells specialize
on parts of the philharmonic whole.

IV. Blue Fin in the Seas of Hemingway

So we have a blue-finned
chance and slow light
with gold of the horse's mane
streaking across the fire door,
heavenly payloads of Friday
with holes opened in being
present, where the petroleum
engines explode, running
chief ruminations off as fast
as possible in whitewashed
conference rooms at high noon.
No one could envision the Earth
without the many incomparable
flights of birds, without tactics
of jays or intelligence of the cells
which is beautiful and urgent,
expressed in design of the body
transformed by consciousness
lifted on wings of the sciences.
Deny this, then we welcome you
to the current-day dark ages.
If they're viewed in fast forward,
the plants can be seen deciding
which way to grow, as they appear
to be moving like stringy animals,
as if a further day now calls us
for so much that lives inside us
under the blue fin in the spine,

and so much that surrounds us
alive where the brain was designed
by systems of cells to be university
of the body, to invent the mind
as representative of the cells
not only so we'll hear sticks
cracking but the morning raga.

BEFORE SUMMER

All morning, punctuating our talk,
workers have been feeding Oregon trees
into a yellow grinder.

> In the neon-lit cafe before finals,
> another person at a wooden table brags
> she doesn't like poetry.

> Later, in the night gymnasium,
> hundreds of lights flood a man
> jumping into the open.

In the locker room, a beardless man
undresses— his back, shoulders,
and chest thick with glistening blond hair.

> A small woman in a long flowered skirt
> tells how she escaped Vietnam
> in a small boat on the ocean.

BAY OF LIGHT

The flux which is quick finches, standing cedar, red-violet neon script,
the furnace fired up in vaults back in the past, which is present,
the glide of commons stretched butter-yellow off putty-knifed prow,

the sun tendering cells alive, body resounding where sense unlocks,
the electrical cells that curve with the current moment of sanctuary,
the rain on the roof, river, moving through matter, making it move,
the evening that holds within solidness of morning that breaks,
the canvas shore cross-hatching behind, spinning a blue churn,

the light in the spiral glass bulb taken on by the breathing room,
the hatching sea bass beginning where the ocean rolls in turning,
the crimson beige that battens slight gull sands as undergo hatching,
the man in warmth of being in a room still learning love beyond love,

the sweeping in of the wind, light entering mind and dark unfolding,
the life of the hearth and shop, life of the road and tall grasses,
the blossom with whole Saturday opening, cherry within scent,
the path that will break into parts and reassemble the moment,
the carrying wave able to break around a stone piling then rejoin,
the spliced downdrafts on commons blanched and carved in fractals,

the light of Thursday streaming, light which is still where it has been,
the next scent of orange, taste of lumberyard dust from the saws,
the alto down-worked root that presses, glowing into the reasons,
the roads with their miles and without, seeing what shows or not,
the heights that unravel over further dark purple seawater depths.

READING THE AIR

The more speechless incompleteness has been,
the more ancient the fern imprints in winds,
the more panthery the raw insistence of hunger
in the slow motion of a naked human shoulder,

with surf-breaking risks under cataclysmic stars,
the slumber-shot prime widening in a root-held
shiver on the proving grounds of sleep-shelled
providence, while exquisite instruments resound

between innate conception in the rake of Rothko
red-violet reds and plum-wrestled scarlet dark,
the way fir needles drop and more of them form
dedicated to the beautiful mother of consciousness,

given the pulse of a body in space, shape of bones
in the chest, the inherited tongue and ancestral jaw,
the shoulders and new brain lifted by neighborhood
crows around which fern-raked evenings can heal.

The compass eye sees the apple continue round
and electric as agile hands of an East European
concert violinist, the rain falling broken and whole
through the spectrum uncountable lives from now

the unfinished hour already leaving as fresh water,
camouflaging absence when a tiniest seed sprouts,
sunlight holding it in emptiness with little to lose
where esoteric antennae defy quick explanations.

BEING CONTINUES TO BEGIN

The root wheel revolves on its ring of the equator where cellular beings began. At what point did sleep-swimming wake?

In split-second Celsius weave, long hair falling across bare shoulders.

An orchard paw sinking as it lifts into ongoing fractal turns.

Redwood groves combing the spectrum, carrying eyes into heights.

Little in the present seems different or the same before winds edit it into the documentary film of ancestral forgetting. Galaxies appear swirling in Van Gogh's daytime sky, and spreading through the aurora borealis of Emily Carr's sky, when the nature of glaciers melting is to become what never was.

Light splashes through nutrients of corn as arboreal mycelia sweeten in elastic time.

At the beginnings of speech, fossil curves in gravitational matter have scarlet dark softening lips on lips.

Once the shaman's face appears before a person who suffers, is it the place before anything's happened?

Has anything we've done been other than collective? Is this the only road we could be taking? In the history of mercy, what happens next?

THROUGH THE DOOR TO WHERE THEY WERE

What crimson does is how crows show up in their black-winged tribal robes. As sad as grain is, an arm exposed to sun at a feed lot will absorb it. The bright hemispheres making crow landings follow their findings. Flashes of archaic dust shift when a mammal moves or we're parts of one another. At the edge of the hour, the eye's taken to where it begins dissolved in fir forests and heavy sea-moss, where the rock of open air hasn't been much for the crows.

————

The universe isn't a machine. It doesn't need fuel; it is fuel. But say it's a machine. It doesn't need its parts. It doesn't need to work or lie to labor or management. When a person eats a slice, parts of the pie transform. A shoe isn't the sidewalk or a hammered-down maple hallway. A country isn't its border as the border isn't a country. A carpenter's level shows arc, the way voice reveals light. A carpet isn't comfortable, the way light doesn't reach the brain, only its resemblance. The briefest solidness on Earth has forever been empty. A hard brevity falls upon fields and rain forever.

————

The people we know may be making their way back through aspen leaves. What's built up steam will be falling whether or not it's more exact. Intuition that learns to live in the collective will inherit increasing complexity. The impact of thumbs pressures what evolved from the first tall Argentinean poplars. Red-orange will ponder almost always in waves. To live here is to grow between cultures of 7 to 8 billion people.

—————

Is this a place that goes to work each minute? As smooth as the teeth of the rain, mammals and grasses sink root. Ancient worlds that made us, from before the concept of beauty, should ultimately be able to survive us. Where beginning's rooted in imperative, mind grew once the sun poured into green repositories of the unscrolled leaves. After a great long time and the conditions above have improved, future archeologists will be brushing soil from a few white bones of ours, maybe lifting out a console radio or Boeing 747 fuselage.

—————

Is that the roar of blurred props of an antique lighter-than-air ship? Aren't these the centuries that refuse to be held down for anything? When pilots were no longer able to hear their own engines, did they know where they are? Are babies on Earth being born hungrier every moment? Has enthusiasm of Manifest Destiny exceeded demand, and did the supply of alluvial splendor pan out? Are mountain-top miners dumping mounds of toxic ash into valleys for the place to absorb the same species as we are? Could we stop wheeling out whoever's determined to put us at risk? To the naked eye, aren't live animals an electroluminescence beyond measure?

—————

Isn't this the place where angels once were believed so prevalent they were known to dance in pinwheels on the head of a finishing nail? Do we always have to be transmutations of genetic markers, releasing a little of what the wind grasps? In the wilderness replete with urban sprawl, can faces be read as books? Can't soups have trouble keeping up, given how symbiotic the projects of cells have been? Without our noticing, could confusion over our place within ecosystems have infiltrated how we love?

—————

Grace may be a way of moving aligned with the means of knowing, as if survival of our species weren't only hinged on tools, but beauty and art. A vivid beauty reaches us, streaming light into us, firing up how we first longed to live as beings on Earth. People know a little more than what they'll admit, where honesty isn't just the story spoken in a lower voice. Naked efficiency breeds more than a hoarse-sounding dialect millennia old in its signaling. Open air quickens for anyone not one of the boulders at the bottom of water.

—————

Our tables chained to mountainous night, wheeling chants of masters turn on the taproot of noon. Meteoric New York City moves gyrating in bursts of atomic reformation have their oil-lamp right whales swimming along the continent at unknowable depths of millennia. We've come here dog-dreaming morning and long hair fallen on magnetic shoulders, after how much bulk inclination. In the elder beauty of stone is the first kind face that planted a root beneath the mind, under a few hundred feet of snow.

—————

Bach played on two keyboards at once makes graceful Dakota wind turbines possible. People nearby can be speaking for something missing, ancestors in the calendars, heel clicks echoing in basement halls downtown. The hour of day needs to go nowhere. It shows up in an old hat, surprised even by its bread cooling on top of its mammoth-tusked hearth.

AVENUE OF FALLING RAIN

Evening rain soaks the roof
and small businesses,

East European sailors lumbering
their talk from a portico,
a person in the brick alley wearing
a few overcoats, shivering
in a streetlight's gray-silver rain,
the doorway boarded up where she stands.

Now it's the back entrance to a barn
where she worked when she was a girl.

Night neon from markets glares
and melts through speeding glass,
the news sedans on oily monetary overpasses
under which dirt angels live,
the coffee shops glowing in the uneven dark,
the sky heavy, the way someone's arms
have more stone in them as she sits.

Now the antique rust-brown steel bridge is lit
with candles— no, the glare
from headlights— the voices washed down
Morrison Avenue before they're heard.

A woman slices an orange open
at a table in her kitchen with the small
phone smashed against her ear.

A long-haul rig roars out into the rain
its silver trailers gleaming, its engine harmonic,
purple hot gasoline energy crawling the wind
through leaves in a shudder.

YELLOW CANDLE

Even in a small room
the candle detects wind.

Maybe part of the wind the flame registers
comes from Marion Anderson's '41 *Ave Maria,*
the immense statue of Abraham Lincoln
at the top of the steps behind her.

Current global measurements
cannot be ignored, and yet the yellow
canary still sings his melody with clarity.

The darkness ahead isn't how it used to be.
Oil drums dry up in dusty warehouses.

The candle's elegant shadow
projected onto the wall
becomes a castle lit on the inside,
the room where Henry V
stopped being a warrior.

Tapping cosmic sound, the kingdom
of song birds does not break
into homicidal war. Balanced on curves
of Earth, the canaries we need
to keep breathing are with us still,

with hunger in lifting brightness,
hunger in opening mineral sense.

Medieval shadows flickering on the wall
here in the room, the furnace works
steadily enough, while the wind's driving
more rain from rocks
of the furious coast
against these bungalows.

HALF PATH

A little light goes
a long way
into the blank look someone has
in the line at the espresso counter.

The men unloading new car tires
sweat and sometimes shout across
the warehouse in the chemical half-light.

A woman behind the counter
appears to be breathing colors
of the painting she has going at home,
the one with reds and purples and black lines
casting formal shadows
into the way the things feel.

Once the boy looks into the face
of a wild raccoon, he doesn't feel
quite the same about road kill.

Men unfold tables at the shelter,
and dogs turn their heads from the wind
of one century to another.

A sweater goes out
from someone
into the life of another.

LUNCH FRACTALS

Rain rings and snaps on the stove pipe
    echoing the sky down
into the pizza room where we wait
    after the week's slag and ground swell
that breaks, through turning day on the back
    of night, the call that vanishes
into February where this break has gone
    as if something could be said
but more has gone before, the guy
    in red running shoes could share
what we ought to do with the sky.

What will future people burn in their engines?
    This room has lifted as it waits for others
to enter, some relief from hunger around
    the world, and how does it reach us?
Green peppers plant the green, the young women
    women vanish and reappear, and the father
with two children guides them outside
    into the blustery afternoon, a new group
of workers places orders, in this place
    where orders are taken, this place unmoved
from its hour in '71 – the pinball anthem
    from The Who for those who didn't know
what happened to what we once believed, far back,
    it's playing now with psychedelic posters
I can see now, glowing on the wall their imperative
    half-hallucinated out of fluid colors.

As for me, I'm back pondering that time the Port Clinton
    Police pulled us over in a snowstorm
then ordered us to follow them to the police garage
    where they stripped the old Ford
down to its parts – taking hours – the fenders were off
    and the seats had been placed
on the garage floor. It was urgent, they said,
    they were looking for illegal drugs,
they said, by removing main parts of the engine.
    When they finally decided to reassemble it,
they shrugged and grudgingly put the seats back in.
    Where were the drugs? Students in 1971
were supposed to have drugs, especially if they're driving
    cars a few years old. What they found
by unbolting and removing the muffler was the muffler.
    And what they found were the old fenders
and the dash from 1955, and seal of the muffler
    to the engine, which they left leaking
into the cabin, knowing we planned to drive home.
    And what they found in the grocery bags
were wrapping papers cushioning Christmas gifts –
    when, appearing tired and disappointed,
they declare to us we can go. The roads now are caked
    with ice, and the snow's been piling up,
when we notice clouds of exhaust are fuming up
    into our faces. So we crank the windows down
though it's bitter cold, and the motor's been thrown
    out of whack. Anyway, who gave them
the authority to search us at all? But it wasn't as bad
    as what happened to students not far away
when the National Guard open-fired to disperse
    the rally protesting the war, killing a handful.

And it was better than what happened to friends
        who were clubbed by "riot" police
in a city park in Portland. We have to make it
        maybe 45 miles. If only the headlights
weren't dimming. And I think they stole my compass
        and the concrete our car was driving on.
The snow pouring down carries shapes of the body.
        People are out there in the breath
we share, there are feet that need their footing,
        this hour here has it in all directions,
here in the restaurant with its surfer poster
        showing a man riding swollen waves
he can only intuit, but couldn't possibly see
        rising out of unknown oceanic forces,
lacking the perspective this photographer had
        when she captured the moment, the man
on a surfboard, the dark wave breaking behind us,
        the short time we're here, thundering
and streaming in a long receding wave, where we are
        dependent on our balance and yet free
from the long past forever, almost in the center
        of mind, the Mandelbrot image unfolding
as infinity explored, Did you see it? on the tiniest cusp
        another image of the whole system
bursting with force, asking for peppers, breathing
        within our ways of asking, the motion
of wheels moving the place ahead, with the weight
        that keeps arriving, making us ready.

SONGS FROM FAR BACK

I. Sunday

The stone floor is not enough.
The early garden is not enough.
But the wind is part snow,
and grass, and wild apple.
I cannot think of the end of wind.

II. The Next Key

In the tunnel of doors I stopped
for the wind was carrying the next key
of black light swinging on the chain
of each breath, locking this way,
locking back, locking us into our hope.
And the steady drone from horns of mud
forming underground said there is nothing
we can do. There is nothing now.
The next key is gathering in the mouth
of a squirrel and passing sleekly
down the cat's backbone.
It is like something moving now
in one of the trees.

III. Tongues

Tongues try to save us.
They are mossy fires
strengthening our teeth.
They are soft spades scooping out
dusty waters of a voice.

Later, they return to a field
where a dark ruby sheds leaves
and husks into a prayer.
It is as if we are listening
to the flute of some star
deepening in bones of the face.
Tonight the tongues deepen
in arcing quiet sound chains,
in violet undertow and locomotion.

IV.   Divisions

Early sun plows through heaven.
Bones break in the moon's radio.
Wheels of the bitter aluminum
crash at the earth's husk.
Our dream wobbles, like an ox-cart
we pull but cannot see.
Bare oak pump our breath
as our lungs melt into the sky.
The colors of a face
shatter off the canvas.

V.   Song from Before

Think back to before
we could speak —
the music of water harps,
cornets of sun breaking into riffs,
the brass roof hammered twice,
once in the morning,
once in the evening,
struck hard until it bled
when the bone flutes turned,

wriggling through loose soil,
floating, in the night.

VI. Memory of the Birds

Above the baby bed, the plastic birds
float more perfectly than something
from inside my mother's eyes.
They have come from places far away
I might remember, entering their colors
nearly the first time, moved
by how they undulate and sink
overhead like beautiful magnets.
As if many people shared a love,
they're gliding so clear of each other,
tied to the distance. Perhaps my father's voice
is lifting us out of the muscles, singing
like the scent of spaded ground,
the windows open one evening,
never to entirely close.

VII. The Flutes

In the month when fields are submerged
in blue-black water, when each page
of print has turned dark, people
who love will be steady lamps.
Even cold nights of the year
will not stop the mountain flutes.

VIII. Distant Weather

Our instructions
overturn like sun spots.

There is more, before supper:
the gentle queen repeating
her spontaneous vow, the carbon
with its briefcase of dying plants
and friends, the serious scrambling rope,
other suns, the grief of coal
disappearing out from beneath us,
the stairway of hydrogen,
the onyx thought impacted
in the animals' sun, and not at all.

IX. Memory of the Carnival

Driving in the green Ford,
someone is talking.
The windows are water.
We listen to Grandpa's voice
I think through the radio,
the amber radio light, colors of the dusk.
Outside in the park, all the lights
begin chasing themselves like horses
or fish jetting through the sky at night.
Suddenly animals we have never seen
run out of the trees with their faces
burning. Maybe they're gathering
at the city park, their fur oily
and electric in the music,
with people shouting, burning
machines loaded with people,
tractoring the huge wheel
through the sky and ground,
mulching the huge garden.

X. The Edge

I stop at this edge –
the sky of red lightning,
thunder of the mountains.
And plant my feet inside each step
which becomes a field of snow.
And plant my face tasseled
as wheat flaming in the stomach
of a mountain goat. I want to explode
in a cry, like any bird: Crow.
Hawk. Blue jay. Sparrow.

XI. Trees

All around us, trees
with extended powers
are breathing – the five-winged
maple, jagged tongues of ironwood,
fish-shaped leaves swimming
over the cabin, trees moving
their one syllable that enters
every cell alive – the open faces
of oak, visible ghosts of elm,
talking ash, trees whose lungs
have kept turning inside out,
whose brains have unfolded
into evening and morning sky.

XII. Harbor

Candles still move
through these rooms, breath
still rocked by wind
of our birth, still rising
from its lake of blue flames,
still the first touch of the mother.

APPLE

The edge of the apple's thinking
why shouldn't everybody get a bite.

The dark road doesn't have to go very far,
speaks up the center of the wheel.

A blue jay flies between two immense waves.

We used to be worms of the cross
between the one and the other.

Imprints of ancient ferns
shake the imprint of wind.

The empire of shakes
remains the castle of rocks.

When the apple's eaten,
still the apple's round.

I'LL SEE YOU AT THE CONCERT OF DOVES

I'll see you this evening when the city floats in safety lights
that are jewels retrieved from winds and lifted from tides.

And I'll raise you shade with flashes of tropical canopy at risk,

where free parrots display deep color not seen on the road,
parrots with feathers that are indestructible, given to elevations.

There are people you've known from before you've met them,
people you've seen you never expected close to the old oaks.

I'll see you in the long afternoon in your saffron overtones
and raise you nearby animals teaching how to speak in song,

which is why I'll see you watching over the original colonies
of microbes along fungal mycelia that serve smallest root hairs

and raise mineral circuitry for the mammoth cast of characters
in the tragic play that turns out to be matter making us up
on the rigorous journey completed by individual consciousness.

When reasoning out the wound from the moment of birth,
how often is there intent in what's almost been unconscious?

A single life on a pilgrimage, light of the sun in high grasses,
mother ground, and steps of stone like nobody in the sky,

I'll see you in your liberty with camaraderie and loneliness,
trees that are persons, and undone catastrophe in the sky.

II.

The brain is like a muscle. When it is in use
we feel very good. Understanding is joyous.

— **Carl Sagan**

Think about our dilemma on this planet. If the expansion of consciousness
does not loom large in the human future, what kind of future is it going to be?

— **Terence McKenna**

SEATED AT THE TABLE

Around the lion-clawed table of day and night sit the first humans and their legendary offspring. Given the number of sensibilities and ways they encoded the world, not many can agree about what's to be eaten and how it must be served. Erstwhile, enclaves attempt to enslave escutcheony legions that qualify as *the other* to do the dirty work.

Ten thousand and more religions and cults undertake rituals, while a hundred thousand elevated orators, priests, kings, sales executives, jokers, and great mothers deliver life-changing addresses to the collective.

Drink, psychoactive fungal mash, joy and agony, curiosity and retrograde amnesia, on top of stone-serious harping and military-escorted sewing circles flaring up in choral renditions, sports enthusiasts roaring out lion prowess, adventurists snapping back the continuum, daughters with ox carts crossing the city limits— these and many continents more abound.

At the table are log-thumpers and transcendental Trappists, army experts in snare and stretched-skin comrade carriers, founding fathers of conga and great mothers of tabla Sanskrit, with stick-wielding unrestrained rhythmists, cymbalists, and triangle trainers bursting past colossal stone figures at the borders of longing. Who can tell where anything ends?

You can see kind presence and formidability, feuds and armored vests, lingering desire and visitations of suffering, with hunting and contemplating, everyone with a full face and refined head, including those who were ostracized flat, wearing scarlet bonnets or hair stubble shirts with those who'd never sit without standing, alongside those who couldn't help but join or refuse. Whoever was born is there.

THE BRAIN AND ANIMALS

The brain loves its many animals,
which can be something
that the mind immersed
in wall-to-wall people may forget.
A manta ray flying in along reefs
of coral speaks the brain's language.
Maybe the mind over a big meal
has banned animal references
in an effort to spotlight the human,
maybe to maximize profit,
but the brain making up dreams
stands up for its allegiances.
One night the brain kicks open
the furnace room fire door,
setting the coal-black panther loose
in halls of the old grammar school
when the children are starting
to arrive from their neighborhoods
of morning. And yet what choice
does the mind in the dream have,
other than reacting, experiencing
an adrenaline infusion of fear
for lives of the kids? A wet grizzly
snagging a river salmon turns
to the camera, roaring, reaching
a paw the size of your head

toward the mind, that, terrified
by immense forces bearing down
on its smallness, refuses
to go blank, and breaks out
of the underworld into waking.
What was just going on?
Where am I, and where have
I come from, to wake up here?

GRASSHOPPER CLOUDS

When the mind decides to assume responsibility, rock-bottom hungers may clash.

Demands this desperate may try driving animal trucks unconsciously into one another's headlights, intestinal muds redefining power from genetic undersea horns, filming the documentary from a raven's perch through the eight coordinated eyes of jumping spiders, issuing manifestos on veils of tears.

While mindfulness establishes residence, grasshoppers with serious red veins can be swallowing pain, chewing on meadows, great inhaling swarms on skeletal wings voting yes or no, darkening the western sky before vanishing.

So the tips of billions of tongues lick the instant exhausted, as the next instant rolls undetectably in from behind, to where the next tips of tongues erupt, to taste what's unferned.

From compass cores of becoming, vibratory forces push in fast forward, with mind parking its maneuvers in slow-motion root-hold pull of having a life.

In splashes of overflow light, autonomous breeding wheels. No matter exists but what's already turned into historical antecedents.

Over time, zero plus zero approaches one, but who will be here to see it? Boot-black echoing is echoing in stem-cell shadow fallen flat and full through the unfilmed emergent communications of specialized cells.

YARD CONTROL

A blood-crimson and brown rooster shrieks and pecks at hens when the hour to do this is now. He scrutinizes the positions of nests and state of the yard before deciding to yodel, calling out their location there in the canyon of so much unknown.

This time, he succeeds in throwing himself into it, crowing up further alarm over the tradition, demanding the protectorate remain alert, that all chickens watch for daytime terrorists or unguarded panthery assaults from the perimeter.

He points the head on his neck at the sky out of view, aiming so high up he's out there with satellites, crying out there's no excuse not hearing. He stretches and flexes his wings and bulk in the assumption he's more than you'd expect, maybe two or three at once, or unnaturally gargantuan.

Finished with this, he looks down at his feet. Maybe he's tired, but he seems sad, walking behind the hen house like someone's uncle whose dog hasn't returned.

Now he's tending to the lay of feathers, reassuring his muscles and bones, taking a break from his burdens when he can, since the job of upper management can be relentless, though you'd never trade it for anything else.

BREAKING OUT OF THE PEN

The rooster running the compound in back of us may be tough on the roost, but he's punctual and unwilling to surrender. Of course, warding off chaos has never been easy.

For whatever reason, whether fed up or hungry, a determined hen decided to widen the gap under the fence. Maybe she pictured eating well or breaking out of the pen, escaping the autocracy or incorrigible pecking order. When the hole was ready, she dove under and made a run for it.

It may have been political, since others who'd had her back followed quickly. Up close, these chickens weren't in bad shape, and didn't look afraid. Nearly as tall as young kids in the neighborhood, they looked at us, adjusting their binoculars, a camera crew in the yard, preparing to film the documentary.

A moment later, they were off like ostriches, racing to perimeters and back, calculating measurements, before sprinting north through the next yard then across the road, whistling off in a frenzy, as if no one could see them and no one would know.

RISK OF YES OR NO

The sea-lion dives through lost wrecks of breath in the sum of parts,
the primitive political rabbitry within tiniest decisions of microbes,
the bottom-fished stops of sea that employ two eyes, leveling churns

where brown pelicans fly between the sweet wood porches of cell walls,
the fragrances of dusk-draining heat for seven billion people at once,
the undercovered flounders in extravagant remains passing as thought,
the fervent ocular space exacted through belief in the invisible gases,

the hawk risk of everpresent no or yes, fruit that repairs into repast,
crustaceous ongiving roosts alongside infinitesimal neuroleptic slopes,

the purring of mountain bats where great grandmothers of cells are
howls smoking with our risks to ongoing life, outmoded endlessness,
much that has gone off into generational heaves, swinging the place
like a battle ax, the forward onrush of origin undergoing new floods,

muscular mathematics surrounded by tortoise crawls in uncertainty,
wasps flying a laser conundrum through their share of eradication,

the last ultra-blue spectrum hanging on to difference or similarity,
the historical carbon in a horned moth's wing of future adaptation,
the inherited purposeful complexity within one another's seawater.

RETURN BEES TO PLANTS ON THE PLANET

Bring back the symbiotic thrill
from when power-clawing life
off of the offshore seafloor
was outlawed by common sense.
Oil cardinal elevators of identity
in this age sitting on its aquafers.
But restore the greater undone
for the sake of the indivisible
pollinators and keep choosing
to begin once more unpolluting
and improvisatory with Grandma's
bins of potatoes, before light splits
into its future high-rise farms.
Let coal-fired histories be erased
by the high tide. Re-establish
refined aesthetic contemplation
as the top of the wheel returns
to the ground and water thunders
in the falls. As fluorescence deflects
downtown, blending into a blur
in the city, restore Teddy Roosevelt
to his national forests in the middle
sound of the species. Return viable
composites, eyes filling in matter,
and a viable future to the present.
Return native gulches, illustrated
monastic first letters with a slam
of the screen door into its frame,

where day-to-day practice learns
to be energy's bread. Return
the voice that speaks with lift
of small ribs of a barn owl.
Restore mineral shimmering
to the bearings of hosts
behind the black iron gates.

NUCLEAR SUN

I. Hieroglyphic Dust in the Air

A barn collapses and fills again with wind
and light over the little ant. It's like breathing,
the scarab beetle scrambling along an edge.
And God must be riding a horse made of wild energy.
And that horse probably eats grass out there
at the far reaches behind the black mask of the rainstorm,
where the trees made from bones are still standing
and the mushroom rings and the celery tastes.
"Wake up, little brothers," the moon says to its oceans.
Isn't it like that, the sun centering in space of each atom,
in space of the spiraling, saucering galaxy
much larger than the Milky Way, with dragonflies
that pulse with stars for their bodily atoms
flying the first creation this is?

II. Walking Beneath Cottonwoods

Hours before leaves begin, we walk under cottonwoods
at night, a few scattered stars letting us be here,
trees holding as roots in the air, in the split second
of eternity, for what do we know that isn't from before
speaking? Isn't it all the tree's body, the space between
branches, the light reaching from roots and shade-fall
parts of ancient buildings that left imprints on the day?
In a house nearby, a girl's sleeping. When she's thirty,
she'll know how to move unlike any other, in her way.
Things won't be easy. She'll need to be stronger

than anyone she knows now. The roots of the air
are ready to break into rain. But why would God's horse
be thirsty and hungry? You could say both God
and the horse would be hungry due to all the blinding
blue blazes of yellow-gold suns so white and empty
then impossibly red. The cottonwoods are being
alive in waves of light from the Earth and space,
when someone you love talks and moves closer to you,
and while you're talking, you want to tell her.

III. Afternoon Lit by Breakers

This afternoon lifts and releases
night into day, igniting the open sky
over the oceans. It breaks over us
in waves on the surface of bean leaves.
The cottonwoods press powerfully
through root roads, using the gravity
of starlit snowfall through atomic core
centered in planetary heat. In the churning
and heaving, what might have fallen
years ago gives in again to what this is,
propelling cool downswings then pushing
certain old doors slowly open as we work
for the harmonics of wood and crickets
that live in the hollows of what's said.

IV. Morning Sun

Blossoms burst out of their buds in the sky,
from within the lift of their branches,
the midnight emerald of leaves, if you will
be starting over, trying to hope into the sun,

if you will be bathing in sun for the cells
of your body, sitting cross-legged at the coast
of breath with the lift of your spine, the sun
in every molecule, the morning sun rising over
the future, showering light, showing the road.
And so Bhagawan Das sang in his muddy locks
before oceans, where waves of his instrument
could reach over footpaths that guided him
as they do us, in the ancient story when atonal
stellar sky is giving way to dawn within cells.

WITH HEAT GOING UP

Nothing that goes on around here
was bound to. Morning, evening,
standing up and walking, it all
depends on forces out of control.

Mammoth wealth has always weighed
more than it's capable of handling.
It slam-dances glutinous gigatons
in acid-drenched high-end mosh pits.

So you'd like to leave a brief message
for people thousands of years out.
Nothing on Earth continues to exist.
Do we know people will stay people?

The eyes that work within the mind
see that they have little choice
but to signal hello and goodbye
on a split-second speck in infinity.

What's the rush or drive to victory?
The heat's going up in the stir-fry pan.
No species is capable of wiping out all
microorganisms, just the world it knows.

The night high with wheeling galaxies
falls on all fours through the day.
Day does not exist in outer space.
The mind stops when breathing ends.

HAVING LESS

Seen from the future, how much
of the present can you count on?
What's everything you might want
if it doesn't support the common good?

What's all that you've worked for
if it undermines equity between
generations, or puts more guns
in hands of those who believe in fear?

If you can no longer cut into meat
without seeing the heart of the animal
pumping blood to every animal cell,
if you can't separate the mother and calf

without harming yourself over time,
can you release your hand, teaching it
another grip that will hold you calm?
Every year hatches incendiary songs

that leak through splits in the second,
diving in beyond us, to parachute
with bioluminescent jellyfish in waters
fighting dark centuries of disappearance,

but can we see more than here and now?
Can we plan the way living cells choose
to sit with a bowl filled with the forest
as birds fly for the grasses and fir trees?

SALT ON THE TABLE

I.

The count of suns in the night sky
resembles the number of bodily cells
looking together through the eyes,
where unanswered thirst crystalizes
into salt. In mint soils of a chance
operating in the back-roar, sea-pulse
turbines roar, sweeping people on
past the point of resistance, as global
water falls across the eons-long saltlick
spectrum uncountable lives from now.
Camera-phoned cities of comprehension
linger in the morning around café tables,
each of them with a glass shaker of salt.
Maybe the root roar's been elephantine,
disquieting for desire, where the body needs
a future that could actually appear. Brands,
broods, boxes, 20 lb. bags, and canisters
of sodium chloride appear in rooms refined
for camouflaging the bitterness of old meat
or spiking our coevolved vegetable gustation.
So a container of salt will someday be lifted
into the air by archeologists centuries off.
Someone nearby will know salt used to be
a form of money paid to Roman soldiers.
Or no one will be there, trying to dig us up
only to find, on ruined tables, salt sparking

the way it has on our tongues, down the road
from modern sea brine foaming as something
ancient in the lot of people who've realized
severity crystalizes, while gentleness flows
with what reinvents us now out of glacier
melts that keep feathering back slowly
into wholly incontestable salt-rich seas.

II.

Lifting light in the offshore kelp-forest swaying
guides more eyes to overhead edges of water.
Membranous clutches of tiny eggs hold on out
of sight, beneath lengthening-long flashes of leaves.
One of the more spiny big-faced fish has left them,
back in time, where eyes and tail-turns follow
out sea-salt torque in strata of dark-blue sound.
Resolution wakes out of origin. Multiple rivers
in the undersea swirl. Immense circulation leavens
conception. Contemplation wheels on billions of stars.
No wait – on billions of galaxies. Under great night
weight blooms and blisters facelessness of fossil-aching
out in spiral shape. Ancient cold and warm, melting
of motionless freezing heaves, the mineral skeleton tills
ringing in unfinished ringing, unfolding through moves,
waves weaving upon more underneath waves, coves
going on filled, emptiness of the light drawing back
on sense. The undersea surf aims, concentric shores
break in the indivisible roll, what an egg's making
of its seed takes knowing jolts, fluid and buoyant
upon dark matter, which is hunger that tastes of salt.

III.

"where respiration itself mingles w/ mystical blue salt that understands
itself as vibrational arrangement knowing its essence to be spawned by
spontaneity" – **Will Alexander**

The human shoulder rounds off,
is well rounded, prepared
for refined reception of the head
of another wanting to lay
its burden down, to rest in a place
away from punch-clock hours
circling over or tightening
a throttle around the equator
where species exist that have never
been found in root-searching
heaves that fill with mineral circulation
to lift with forces powered by gravity
where sinking rains have them
rising overhead, where events unfold
making out of the genome new branches
where leaves open into maps
of the hand under the wide wing
of rainfall sweeping across croplands
in their inveterate light-bending
cloak of however much we're aware of,
that we never could have imagined
when we first learned grammar
in springboard licks of vibration
that indicated what was near or out
of reach, when we thought we could see
the future before us, that hadn't
happened and wasn't fixed, but surely
it would happen, which placed
a serious burden on liberty,
giving us a chance only so long.

SUMMER HIEROGLYPHICS

I. End of the Week

Friday afternoon, chestnut trees heavy with rain
to come, dogs running back to the doors
more quickly. A sudden yard with marigolds
and red-violet unknown flowers, blossomed
out of time, Friday taken back through our cells.

At the lake, distant cranes fly like sticks
over the breakers. Gulls disappear
in almost-visible choppier whitecaps.
Behind us, our jobs have become specks
across fields where the sun rise splintered
into legal words barely making a sound.

II. Unexpected Levitation

A cricket works up its pulse of night.
Waves we've never seen shake us.
Ground grooves where weight goes.
Golden Mean ratios in human faces
are found most pleasing to the eye.

As easily as plants rotate their leaves,
a man's climbing his 1970s ladder
that vanishes under him and above
in slow-motion sky. Dark-green glass
through which the woods can be seen
shatters. What could be left behind
will return in circulation. The weight

of our forgiveness hinges on change,
while what the sun does over the city
in the deep summer, gives more
buoyancy to the waters of cells.

III. Tomato

Here's how one theory explains it:
We aren't just from the earth,
of course, but from solar systems
in the mineral galaxy of electromagnetic
spectra, where the arc of growth
and angle of picking a tomato happen
at once. Knowing when to pick a tomato
but hesitating is like not participating
in the conference due to overthinking how
to ask why it is we don't see ourselves
in one another instantly and irreversibly.

The tomato has come from another planet
to appear here on its stem where it ripens
and we can see its progressive reddening.
Finally, it's the soul that's picked,
the tomato, red and deepening.

IV. Planets Lined Up in the West

In 1954, a locomotive on its evening run
roared past into town, the white-blue
steam blasting out in manes and pipings
from behind the wheels bolted together
into a single visible pumping, the planets
lined up, pulling on the newborn, with words
lost in sound, in steel tonnage, in long distance.

On her porch, a woman touched paint to a bowl,
the amber light around her glowing on leaves
of long willow branches, with dusk over the miles
of alfalfa fields in scent from an open window,
a blue-white sun past the Milky Way galaxy
adding a touch to the cerulean blue she's using.

V. Dark and Light Evening

The dark evening and light evening mixed
and half-light glowed, when the judges
threw out what might not fit their needs.
Houses in the city grew out of people's lives,
from within a held nail or a person's fingers.

When eagled sunlight looked down at half-light,
scampering stopped. The locomotive thundered
day into day, filling the valley, while cliff edges
sent lightning, cutting off words, dust rising up
where the egg in abbreviations was red-hatched.

Brothers before anyone could talk were the birds
and windy tall grasses when becoming themselves,
when mammal breath had a shaded volcanic glow
and man had both woman and man within him
aa woman had both woman and man within her,
when the body knew our origin made this obvious.

Growing up, we've been given over to massive rock
and strike of each step lifting us as we're tied up
in knotted Celtic ropes for our protection from falls,
with a sense Christians were premature about that,
the fall, when sun sets on everyone's intrinsic worth.

VI. Bending with the Road

So the road swerves. Suddenly it disappears then reappears.
It breaks open in cherry blossoms, loses its phone and nerve.
People can be roads that have remained unpaved, and more
like buildings with the sound of sea winds in the hollows

of bones, with a view from the high windows over a café,
just to hear what ends up broadcast on the summer radio.
But you know how hard the road under the sun can be,
and how difficult to fathom the newspapers of people are,
given what goes on behind the scenes. At the river market,
Thai stir fry wafts, as meat slightly stews. New jobs appear,
as do the reasons too many apply: too much news, too much

open-air-market with fried Hawaiian rice scent, German
kraut steam, and Chinese finery in every fresh breath,
too much in what was lost in the hustle of torsos, hulks,
and the weight-garbed populace strolling with new babies.

> *In centers of planetary atoms, in the sky,*
> *we can hear the bending of solar things*
> *en mass – solar atoms, spinal roots of us.*

VII. Down a Telescope's Focus

While the ants channel, salt takes on a dull glow.
Work breaks as late night store fronts hold back
what hasn't been claimed within the human psyche.

The unknown rolls rolls over us with its parallel
pastures and redwoods in everyone's circulation,
with waves breaking in fields of breathing grain,

in the glow of rubies, taste of the Yakima apples,
in the rushing of air that fills people with travel
and talk, where the sun hasn't been given a name.

VIII. Crackling Power Grid

This place, a sunflower seed husk, late in the summer,
this place, a footprint the sun has just left scorched,
while grain cooks up in light and squash plants climb
across the ground, through months around months.

How did this happen, when what leaves is what returns
but is gone, as what lives will be going back into Earth?

The dusk cranks up its platform of high-powered angels
whose bodies are tattooed Southeast electrical stations,
buzzing and crackling with orange evening harmonics.

IT ISN'T KNOWN UNTIL IT IS

Because won't the report on our time here be turning into soil?
Because hasn't the spectrum been spectacular beyond words?

As being evolves in being, the interdependent working cells are sacred.

Has anyone around here turned out to be a declaration of freedom?
As precise as the smallest parts of us have been, aren't we here?

In the late hours of night, the birds which turn ultraviolet are flying
in back of starlight, circling with planetary winds and the equator
that assigns each being an importance equal to that of every other being.

Because it's not well known how a house built into the open arms
of older maple trees promotes peace on behalf of the next generation.

And who hasn't given the self and its ensemble a few paths to liberation?

Aren't ecosystems calling on people every day to ask for stewardship?

Maybe there are variations on visualizing species within an ecosystem,
the way they're distinct and yet always parts of the whole which is alive.

Haven't chords been emerging that no one in history could have heard?

Haven't the lips of two people out of sight touched like nothing before?

Because the calibrated instruments of scientists expand human senses.
Because the experience of matter around us rings, in resonating rings.

As being grows in being, the present systems of working cells are sacred.

III.

The time has come to reclaim the stolen harvest
and celebrate the growing and giving of good food
as the highest gift and the most revolutionary act.

– **Vandana Shiva**

I believe nature is a force of good. Good is not only
a concept, it is a spirit. – **Paul Stamets**

THE SIZE OF A PERSON ON EARTH

At least on one clear night each year,
suns of the Southern Hemisphere
should be visible in the North, so the eyes
of Western supremacy could see where we are,
along the edge of a vast saucering galaxy
we're infinitesimal parts of. If this were arranged,
supremacy in the North would have the chance
to look overhead into the thick body of suns
and matter of our galaxy swept by cosmic forces
around the core. They'd be able to see a wide
spiral cross-section, a cosmic Kundalini spine,
the compass needle used by late night travelers
such as African dung beetles (Scarabaeus satyrus)
proven to rely on it, as well as the sun and moon,
when finding the route home. If the Southern sky
were over the North, Western arrogance could see
Alpha Centauri, the Carina Nebula, and Southern
Cross flaring brightly enough for eyes on this planet
to realize life probably exists on countless planets
and moons, perhaps even on asteroids or comets,
that the way matter assembles into cells, the cells
collaborating establish intelligence, for as it is
on Earth so it must be elsewhere. We evolved
the capacity to prepare for more than we've seen.
The volume on this needs to be loud enough,
given the 7.6 to 9 billion of us that our actions
have put at risk, where consciousness continues
to evolve and the late night sky ought to be
enough to humble anyone, colossal or small.

BIRDWATCHING

An ancestral mother or father
in the human body of cells
and tiniest unnamed beings
influenced by St. Francis of Assisi
back in the day sits slowly
in the interferometric arboretum

where biodiversity thrives and maybe the mind sees
it's home, as contemplation opens for the merge
of Whitman with Merleau-Ponty, as profound would be
the hay-making before you, and the nest weaving
as you keep moving,
                    to up and start, to keep moving
to live by the river of identity, your mind reserved
for what you like over what you hate, as is your right
from before even pre-atonement gun-toting.

As others walk across the archeological observation deck,
they include a bride of fertility whose innate learning presses on
through recent proclivities in their elk rut, with a tall drink
of water winning or losing another ear each time the self finds
Van Gogh in the grip of great need,
                    beside a corporeal voice
engineer for the clock-pulsed stage with a high-end contention
sporting irascible camouflage in musical conservatories
of inception and reconstituted Tuvan shamanism.

An elaborate hee-haw North American innocence pursues its own
instincts, hell-bent on home-schooled mis-under-accuracies
sharpening their ballistic yellow pencils on compunction,
the ash-throated flycatcher in the pock-hunkered purchase
of indulgences from relatives

                              when joining the party of identity
in the neighborhood of a goose-necked amendment distributor
sauntering off hand-in-hand with an attractive premise
of pre-Constitutional bell-ringing honest as oxygen but more
noticeable than a rose-breasted grosbeak by an astute dowager
in the violin-plucked semblance of heat-stroke recovery,

a troubadour black-chinned sparrow whistling
where the news has become too grim
for pronunciation, followed by a number
of flowery orderlies wheeling past a stainless steel stretcher
on which the pale mother of people lies,

                                          under the gaze
of a 34-year-old child employed by the crowd-control
baton and tear-gas battalion undergoing averted miscalculation
that leads to a little warbling vireo, a little wife ushering in
further daughters and pulsatile appositive aplomb

for an exemplary emptiness pedaling abstruse Egyptian relics
as her husband carries out a dalliance, holding the hand
of the human out of aspiration around transudations
of the charismatic animals that doctor punctuality

where a merchant of Vesuvius in a wide-brimmed hat
of star systems completing a beautiful aerial assault
of indifference pushes a stroller of quick-growing triplets

into a mooling chorus of town boys in long white hair
and beards from the mothery Whitman conveyor lines
serving at the pleasure of innocence, if not Ezra Pound,
Demetri Shostakovich, Mark Twain, the Thaumaturge
of Milan, John Dewey, Krishnamurti, Florence Nightingale,
the Sultan of Swat, John Pershing, or infamous cardinals
who pitched for St. Louis, Ram Dass, Marshall McLuhan,
Madam Curie, Woodrow Wilson, or Hildegard of Bingen,

where they are now in the Palace
of Earthly Tranquility written
into the genome back when why care
if you can or can't trust unlike others
to tell you of your long inclinations

leading to a quick swallow of aspirin from a fat linen pocket
in eschatological belief aching for all the quickly damned
underfunded dumb of us
                                while our spaceship circles
the bonfire that draws tree trunks out of their nuts,

above a tribunal judge in a 15th century Florentine cap,
witnesses unsnapping leathers, down to torturous unequal
distribution for the masses, under the balding white eyes
of current trans-Arctic melting
                                where unbridled innocence
of this kind fails to keep its mind unfettered, slugging it out
with the abject other without fear of promulgations
of propaganda as were seen in a ladder-backed woodpecker
or associated with claims of understanding more
than you learned by working jobs and filling
the many meat lockers with artistic renderings

of matter for a mother of us with an honest grip
on the upturned hull in civic mobilization
of Middle C adjusting its pitch for the economy,

applying stores of mis-opprobrium to a crack
of the mule whip in a regal coronet
of evaporating Ice-Age lakes with a taste
for river-soaked bear tracked to the reaches
by a mint-fresh phenomenological leaf-over

whose better effects surmount,
where everything soon enough
must be blooming bright and plumb.

SO LIGHT PLANTS ITS ROOT

I. Bearing the Beautiful Collision in Rothko

Long-held outmoded assumptions
that stocks of materials available
on this blue planet could never be
exhausted, or succeed in swamping
the populations with floods, are still
tender from eggshell digs in the greater
undone, while anthropological cracks
in the continuum warp photographic
eyes over the centuries. The outskirts
have been paved over using contraries
with old-world animals, glistening, rare,
on the screen. And so heaviness has more
than started to frame the freezing hot
whole range of slightest shifts in Celsius
leaching into electric longing and jackboot
fears, redesigning solidity while it falls
out of sync with quick-melting elevations.
At the table, unknowing may request more
servings, drifting over ground-hived bees
at the edges of shape where beings are,
who grew up with belief in the morning
and then evening. For the body seems to
have formed as a consequence of the roar
of vacuum-shattering outer space inflating
after the mysterious split-second ignition
that peaks now in the inherited tongue,

the ancestral jaw, familiar bones in chests,
as we try to grasp the fast-swelling oceans
of archaic languages with in-between colors
generated out of coevolving spiraled codes.

II. In the Room with Paul Klee

Sun as it blazes over the horizon
makes dawn in the primal brain
at one with the emergence of self.
It's the nuclear fusion generator
you could feel at the root of being.

With cosmic rays showering stone
there's quickening within matter,
the mother-seed of consciousness.
No person remains sculpted clay.
No clay's playing the baritone sax.

Dark columns of smoke say wildfire
rides in on electromagnetic pulse
from a future already come to pass.
No person you've noticed in the day
was able to avoid some kind of birth.

The dawn sun in nuclear blazes
appears on the eastern horizon
in every cell which comes to life,
in every form of being created
by living collaborations of cells.

III. Pollock Painting Organic Expression

Given the huge number of other species alive in the human body
where they co-evolved with the organized systems of cells
and contribute now to inner workings we only know expressed,
it's fair to say we haven't exactly been alone and aren't only ourselves.
It happens we aren't exactly separate from all this circulating breath
that surrounds us, and we aren't different from what becomes us,
what becomes of us in leaves and vines, in living alongside 230,000
newborns every day around the world or cradled here in our arms.
For the rain that falls to ground also reaches the blood, with 81,000
unnatural chemicals in air and water also chemicals in the cells,
where anyone's material poverty is also poverty in us, with the living
climate the shell protecting the nut like the skull around a brain,
pollination guarded by husks of grain, bees that are breathing cells,
where we're flying birds in the computer eye, wired with wild reactions,
the work wail populated with herds grazing over soft calls for extraction
to rev up the nectars of summer, that resist completion for the rest
of chaos, with aerodynamic blades generating the new energy still
spinning behind drips and splashes when Pollock moves at work
in old shoes all paint-slopped where the truth's been aimed at gravity
making weight where thinking acts as if we've been here all along,
muscle memory lit from the tiger bones out to the clothes with truth
hungry enough to be both mother and father of the visible music
in indivisible slumps and peaks of philosophic matter off the brush
fallen heavier than trailer trucks of machine-tilled slipstreams turning
over the felt underground with ongoing circulation where we've been
or might have gone with dark and light streaming down fast into arcs
of concatenated sky out in the rain in falling rain that enters the blood
with its pulse of wind in between the poles, with tiger-toothed jewelry

of remote clusters of star birth leaning down into paint off the lip
of a can, while the can floats on the ocean of space separating worlds
in which archaic despair and rhythmic pulse have been splattered over
with onyx blood of the auroch, where the day's been unable to stop
breaking out of primordial space to print the papers of night on canvas
that was resounding under inseparable Pollock from the downpour
in a solid drop of black that condenses destiny or spills growing
synaptic vines that fire *en mass* in conditions that gave rise to us.

IV. The Light in Paintings
of Morris Graves

The long-practiced ancillary past
lifts and falls with overhanging
sprays, cypress and mangrove,
as easily as the strings of spiders
vibrate out of blameless presence
unfastening plumb. So the fingers
of the transcriptionist can move
with mineral precision that leans in
out of Chopin. But we can't know
many footprints the coastal winds
long ago scrubbed. So possibilities
exist, some that are able to dwarf
the natural and human spheres
we know. The ancestors, of course,
couldn't see how small the planet is
as the cosmos expands. The Hubble
telescope happened to photograph
aboriginal light that was impossibly
old in the present. Our ancestors
couldn't see dreaming as the brain
in communication with the mind.
There aren't many ways to locate
archaic existence that eventually
led to our lives. We couldn't have
found half the vandalism left here
by gods. So Morris Graves painted
psychic regions of brilliant bright
yellows teleporting through history.

WRITTEN ON DREAM SKINS

I.

The root of consciousness, a man says
in a chamber with a string quartet,
was created with matter in solar forges.
Current uncertainty glows in golden reeds
by the great lake where dragonflies are
flying iridescent flutes of their spines.
In the morning, in a future that survives us,
everyone in town will be rushing for trains,
as beautiful and quick as the people will be.

II.

A shaman studying his bundle of reindeer
and musk ox skins in Northern Europe
might find what a night's dreaming had done.
Around paradoxical intensities of not being
what you think others think of your being
in the present, one person differs from another.
A pike at the bottom of the lake will be leaving
behind the presence of uncaught pike
in your chest by the concept of solidness.
Consciousness is a tree in the forest we'd want
to avoid clear-cutting, an old tree announces
to the closest giant galaxy wheeling out of view.

IN THE WILDS

The anonymity illustrated in biblical first letters of need,
the biomaterial flues fuming a smallest hand-tended fury
in abundance of sea-flora, given Earth's carrying capacity

for the neocortex always under construction, predilections
in business at each corner wrestling loose into a shimmy
of surgical Moroccan dance, revolving on the gargantuan

gravitational axle of enciphered joy welded onto end-lands
of hungers in a remnant of mammal birth, as suddenness
and sleep rub off on assumed ownership down the street
opposites circle with encephalon-razed Greenland melts

uncaked and cracking out of coastal air with work sweats
and labor, geomantic amygdala, razor-finned translucence
biting its lower lip in another home language, as salt-sea

vastness absorbs krill-burst full-score heaves upon bone
slowness with all parts of us in atmospheric circulation.

INSIDE THE BLOOD, RAIN IS FALLING

Whatever was the matter, globalization
of closeness, the shift in clear words
a mother whispers, the gears grinding
in a rose, rotating in the cores
of sense, the cores of certain poise,
ignorance becoming more what it isn't,
for whatever feels knows, whatever
pains stays, whatever has power,
whatever has being, bearing –
all this will not be here
past a certain point.

Our work isn't easy. Mere leaves speak
in a wind on the back of the neck.
The dark-lit gloves that a boy wears
when he's shoveling in front of the house
are the color of tree bark, in a memory
that we're suddenly walking downtown,
as massive orange sky-cranes carefully lift
beams from beds of rumbling long-haul trucks.

When they're finished , someone will speak.
Work will break through the hour in miters,
firmly housed corners, in fresh lumber
lifted and lowered by ocean waters of labor,
wind screeching from power tools hand-held
on yellow scaffolding made for no place
other. Eventually someone will speak.

Kiss the unconscious back into wholeness,
and whisper with mothers of the clear words.
Feel the sun lighting Earth's shell into being.
At some time, rotate in cores of surviving flame
that the molecules still contain, and we have
within us, with the scent of soil after rain,
sophistry laying out stairways to the known.
There's moss with its soft hold on a building,

and the cry of a mouse caught in a talon,
the shuddered glimmering of purple hair
in musical smoke – all this will not be
lasting, past a point. Not that imperative
drives the color of corn, or the timber
of downward dreaming may be a start-up,
that the Motorola will preach surviving
like no tomorrow, like no return, like no gills
in a deep swimming past, no praise in its poise,
ignorance in intelligence, reaching in grasp,
like asking for a single end to pain. It will not
be long. So on Saturday, does the thunder
in bodies lift and lull as if no one had invented
nihilism? Could a wheeling snap of the tiniest
dust flake cut through the risks we can feel
to help us see the rich color of resonant form
all around us. If you eat an apple, can you feel
red-yellow roundness in tart taste of the fruit?
And will you know more how you'll survive?

It's easy to forget passion of the round oranges,
what they cause in people, the way cherry tree
branches can become overloaded with desire,
with simplicity of design in their blossoms
as scent turns into meaning itself. We know

the speeds at which loss is able to overtake us,
when it can happen quickly but then build
over months beneath us, until the touch of rain
has been fingers, in the tendering slowness carries.
No one knows how the sunlight on your arm
touches you and how unknowing blasts pain you.
Even as loss persists, its hold over you can lessen.
Remember that time back in the hospital bed
where breathing was knowing what links us all?

WIND'S ALWAYS ON THE ROAD

The wind may be more powerful
than anyone with her sleeves
rolled up or anything nailed
to a roof or parked in a harbor.
But it's no good at raking up debris.
It has no idea whether it's celebrating
or in a rage, if it's angrier than hell
at not being everywhere at the same time.
Maybe it was just trying to speak
like the Louie Armstrong face painted
on early maps, just trying to blow out
a word when it found it had no lips
or tongue, and no phrases combining
under the surface of air. It found no
mouth lined with teeth for biting off
phrases. All it's ever had is what it is,
a verb transitive with multiple effects
slipping out of control, flapping, shaking
as if the marriage tent's about to collapse,
leaves bent, stems snapped, mass peeled
like layers of skin off a tropical onion,
pieces of straw shot terrifically fast
as javelins penetrating trunks of trees.
Even if the wind did have a neocortex,
how often would it sit down to listen to you?
Could it even hear us shouting down here,
with parts of it entering the slipstream,
parts of it drilling into granite mountains,

while it's circumnavigating the planet
in armadas of ghost ships, vacant planes,
with energies of resurrected whales, asking
for nothing more than the next place to go?

OUT OF UNFATHOMABLE TIME

So the beauty of Venus has its wildfires
spreading now through geomagnetic
pulse that resounds in the small breasts
of songbirds and rooting down-dug possums.

So Blake gazed, in the glow of genetic indivisibility,
at classical shoulders and the elegant torsos
of translucent mammalian thermal conversions,
while the immense gas giants were luxuriating

in primal x-rays that have never stopped nursing
on cataclysmic creation. The concentric instant
jets ahead on squid-shot sea-depths packed
with waking and sleeping, and fresh remains

still awaiting word, longing to hear, with light
rising as it turns even when it's almost nothing
but grocery aisles and carbonic 6:30 traffic
making the place smaller. Where craving fills

its pea pods with a viable version of the future,
with arboreal rhizome sweetening in elastic time,
it takes sharp curves melting and unfolding
in the unfathomable pollination of Tuesday

for breath heating up to reach theater prep rooms
as lamp-quick bulk reflected off the Himalayas
at the top of thought, which must answer
to the mother of humanity in the sensorium.

WHAT IS MORE

Person whose flesh and bone-core oneness cried out after your birth,

whose occult naming of things may have put those things behind glass,

who comes with continuing shares of misfires and bison-blooded bonds
where the fabric's been slack and yet explosive, solid and self-organized,

but whose cellular systems experience uniqueness within the sensorium,

like the clock-cracking hammer-blow shock over having consciousness,

whose nonmaterial advancement communicates between hemispheres
in the nectarine microbial overflow, where dreamtime chooses not to
stay locked behind steel doors, not with openness of day-into-night sky

or given the long-term fir needles of starlight sewing holes in the topsoil,
sparking lattices, resinking carbon in emptiness that remains a place
of beginning with mind and humbleness in the capacity to sense depth,

person whose mountain flies a red-brown bird through ecosystem-pulse

where the moment defies anyone trying to possess it, or the wind or sun,

person whose higher education was handed down split into disciplines,
if only to give you a chance to put them together yourself, to not forget
your potatoes or Mona Lisa present in negotiations over genetic markers

or the sins from before birth, around cattle looking through
    mammal eyes,
or physicists in a field with the coevolved microbes on which life
    depends,

now that great urgency roars in behind teams of gargantuan diesel
    engines

charging the maw which remains sacred for any long-life self-
    perseverance,

for plum nectar and crimson zero, or naked wings of moths one morning
when floods of yellow bloom on Italian marble of a restored
    railroad station.

A FEW STEPS OUT THE DOOR

Where there's a door, should there be a key? It isn't a problem until Pavlov's doorbell rings. It could never depend on hectares of western Roosevelt forests with trust-busting photosynthetic devices, until it certainly does.

The present couldn't know the meaning of lonely, not when the future is already always visiting with its bag of tropical nuts.

Doesn't the present already know more than enough, more than anyone could keep up with? Doesn't the present have its hands full, where being intact inculcates not only hemoglobin production, but the long-time shock of consciousness to the autonomous systems?

Haven't bison-blooded bonds cried in rooms of birth? Through winds ladling overhead waters, doesn't the compulsive naming of things after people tie up urban phone lines?

Of course, everyone goes back to the same inscrutable mother whose effects quicken in the undone as in the done. So the Wild West willingness to sacrifice beauty in the name of utility originated with whom?

When magical wishing calls back from the horizon, *You still need me there?*, the galaxy's spiraling in space, flaming out of its atoms through suns. Its pulses endow seeds along spiral arcs on the face of a sunflower with dark rooms and flames of suns not in suns but cells.

A FEW SAYINGS UNDER THE SKY

What happens next pushes in from the expanse
as light years go on reaching the metropolitan
middle of unnamed streets. Heat multiplies fast
in the present future: it's clear we never thought ahead
while stillness turns inside out on its galactic candelabra.

Sleep-rooted work doesn't appear intent on stopping
its cast-iron plows turning over time, staying alive
in Theravada emptiness where you can't say we have it made.

Exceptionally tough gristle turns up in the midst of quickening
where something appears to be missing, as rapacious
compunction spikes in the face of unpredictable operations.

Underground carbon maintains its 100% footprint,
far from gargantuan melting sources of ancient rivers
and profiteering in which woe besets other animals.

Eventually, business as usual loses its fear of betting
against people's needs, disrupting civilization
from remote locations, assuming externalized costs
are out there, to be picked up by unknown others.

The 4-to-9-year-old crowd appreciates an unbridled market.
The invisible hand comes down from above, leaving something
heavy on our backs. Could it be what we've always wanted?
If something's wrong, is it the greatest hoax ever perpetrated
on innocent people? In the keeping of time, the beauty
of well-built city zoo rhinos dreads the wind's avocation.

The cut worm doesn't exactly forgive the iron plow.
Under philharmonic unknowable planets and suns,
will splits become whole? Doesn't the neural net move
in sync with the corn-yellow present
and its long-term project of the spine?

NIGHT CRICKETS

Even without some grind of starlight,
the moon's axis screeching out of earshot,

ancestors of breath around here,
pole beans growing first in their seed,

a cricket nearby was making its pulse
reach through plexus of a woman's body,

our galaxy spinning immeasurably slow,
a cricket soothing old steadiness down.

But who knows how it goes when earth is round,
since if we work the ground, then it works us?

Behind the house, crickets rounded the yard
under sky, refracting an insect light of stars,

churring in lengthened grass standing or bent,
crickets churning their quieting bay, the things

around them, that they leave for what is.
The root sound hovered pulse under time

it took, a chestnut branch shaking, a spark back
in a man nearby, cedar sprays just swaying

or not as a workday opens its lifting.
Tautness slowly drew what loosened,

its planet further awake and asleep, talking
largely silenced down, shattered and whole

in singing from low hazelnut branches,
from under broad leaves and inside air.

NIGHT SONGS AND SLEEP

Before the church became a sanctuary, the people involved may have felt trembling through the building's stone walls, when those not with them had finally gotten off the clock and were trying out a little ancestral pulse, perhaps knocking and thumping on a single-skin drum to a few strings or singing at the tavern or back in the hills.

Fathers, brothers, and sisters may have sought strength by chanting the invisible closer, hoping to know more deeply how the inexplicable light was forever and forever sound, as sound as living out days and nights in mystery they'd personalized to keep it more clearly in mind, when so much was anonymous already and so much unexplained.

Apparently they intuited calling the invisible their origin and home was a powerful way to govern the psyche, as well as a kind of solution for the problem of death ending life. They ministered splits that separated one from the whole, from depth of the imagination when it isn't simple make-believe but capable of protecting and healing.

When the unconscious wrote to those who tried to be good, maybe some pronounced it an intervention of what's greater. As the sky has been forever in the night, holding what's familiar with what we can't make out, the mind has populated it with entities reminiscent of people, and received, in turn, night songs and sleep.

EARTH ALIVE

I. This Instant

This instant, not everything
in the public library stands
when the climate we need cooks,
oceans first, absorbing more
cosmic heat. When the manta ray
flies in on undersea current,
it finds the coral reef's bleached,
its symbiosis lost. This instant,
warrants back in the constitution
of society's long-range stability
are light on the surface of water,
breath reaching the body's cells.
Wakefulness has been buoyed up
by electrical pulse causing the mind
to emerge, and the mirror in the mind
to stay filled all night with billions
of stars, galaxies, sitars in cells,
billions of ants trucking loads down
corridors to their underground cities.
Millions of people may be brushing
their ancestral hair between states
rooted in time, before they're lifted
by the extra energy inside the spine
functioning as a channel of light.
All the glaciers found on this planet
are melting into unobstructed seas,

and leopards leap in every drop.
Millions are burning chemistry in rivers
of circulation when the late afternoon
shadow falling across the desk
turns into part of something else.

II. In Rings of Trees

Propagation rolls in the harvested hay
where appearances remain intact
over the inner pre-Christian iron
core of the orbiting Earth that steadies
alterations to the apocrypha of *why*.
So an ancient pitch out of the day
resonates in the mammalian torso
where the horse-thundered air embraces
the presence of each one of us as fact.
For the apple taking on form remains
round for a time in the compass eye,
where it's ringed by stands of old trees
that saved many lives as they do now.
A multitude of eyes in the daylight
have lifted, hoping to feel more alive
with standing rings of resounding chords
in background time where not enough
planning has gone beyond planting
the next harvest where matter is
the mother of space not realized
without presence of the undeniable
beautiful signs of life contradicting
gravity, transmitting speech as song,
form as plums, with care in insects
that tender missing halves in pollen

completing dynamic genetic tension.
So the two gyres communicate
cellular design that emanates
qualities of the incomparable
inheritance which must adapt
to conditions that are played out.

III. Remaking the World

Presence interconnects the live ocean
of knowing, where civilization is
much unfinished work making its way
into watershed fact, one sycamore
leaf, then one leaf, one long afternoon
of global indivisibility, then the next,
the way effort's rewarded by the flow
of water downstream, a gong resounding
from the back to the neocortex front
of the brain in an inexorable subconscious
roar of health filled with capillary lift
and radiance of feathers in the wide-open
peacock tail that hypnotizes those watching
from cells of the body through their eyes.
The way the body moves speaks of forces
in this era with its mountains melting
at elevations only a few have imprinted on
in the sensorium more likely to be witnessing
sea surges of stronger storms than ancestors
knew and taught those who followed,
while the body says that what was made
can be built more intelligently, to run
on power of renewable available waves

while causing far less harm to life
which remains our support that grew
out of the spectrum in multiplicity
we have little choice but to embrace.

IV. Every Feather Shows Nerve

Robert McCauley and colleagues at Curtin U in Perth, Australia, recorded vocal fish in the coastal waters off Port Hedland in Western Australia over an 18-month period, and identified 7 distinct fish choruses, happening at dawn and at dusk.

– **Greta Keenan, in** ***New Scientist***

Our survival flies down the highway
into the uncertain weather, relying
on the mineral ignition in bodily cells.
All the while, the cells have been carrying
indefatigable flames on, under the sun,
exploring where they are for the collective,
in the stay of shape on material ground
and free-range space around us that fills
with presence. But this may be the place
where consciousness stops without notice
to follow its own inclinations, breathing
at the speed of waking in one of the many
neighborhoods, in the forest of lumens.
So cellular flare inherits the one horizon
in optical future tense, where the touch
of a hand opens in electric communion
transmogrified by our human limits.
The western wind enables the deep brain

to work around primordial heaviness
while further heat has stayed in the air,
in circulation that goes on below the surface
revealed by prismed light that distracts us.
It merges, the heat, in heat-pump current,
the mollusks down below echoing interests
of mollusks and rockfish talking rockfish,
the scientists say, underneath our hearing.
So fish have been singing, voicing signals.
Who would have guessed how the seas are
a misshaped gargantuan bowl of chatter,
of singing along communicating arteries
where being explores states of expression
that are living works of the arts of cells?

V. Breath Is the Wind in Blood

Cardinal bearing from far back,
re-emergent in applications
of old tools, stays current in the flow
of water as the deep brain pivots,
filling in the past with emphasis,
now that daylight here's on fire
between the North and South poles.
Possibly only Zoroastrian masters
can translate magical indications
in star charts when people we love
have their mountain glaciers melting
and breaking up at x-ray speeds
geologically, when circulation
of the air itself warps, holding down

more sun. So sunlight's delivering
through sprays of sea-prism identity
when no one in the remote future
could remain someone other,
protected maybe by the elemental
bomb as the continuum deals
the way it does, out of anonymity,
as if to force people into thinking
for the whole, rather than negotiating
with police batons out of extraordinary
meanness, or devoting this chance
to talking it out with the mean.
For meaning consists of ecosystems
in ecosystems running on collaboration
of cells that evolved here from the first
over an inconceivably long sweep.
Through groans of buckling bridge steel
in the future of the sky, the burning
wild eye of Pacific squid watches
down long halls of current water.

SONG

I'll see you your Stradivarius fiddlehead ferns
and first red bird in the body before thinking.

And raise you a foundation of salmonberries,

you in your Himalayan throat-singing overtones
combed by the years of Swedenborgian hair
you've brought to negotiations over the future.

I'll see you this evening your last grave of horses

and raise your quantum radio of restorative sciences

where the sea-eagle beak a long time back cracked
through the camouflaged shell of weathery unlasting.

When I've searched through my hands, I've happened
upon fields of your liberty and shade, the savannah
where the lion shakes his gold mane in thermal reports,

where your calf has had milk you've made rich and lean
with mineral-brine rain and vegetables of high resolution,

with animals watching over the future a thousand times song.

Trust my intent, while purposeful, stands humble along trails
of ants tying the freefall underground down with their marks

of a brewed mix of wet (R)-2-dodecanol on the planetary surface where they've drug the sting, communicating through their arts of scent conditions in the colony and nature of their foraging.

Trust that flames enough exist to light candles in every leaf unfurled from the seed that carries the plant to green pastures.

Song is the language that bridges the gaps between animals.

I'll see you your oneness in amber light over steps in a pilgrimage thousands of miles back within octaves. Om Mani Padme Hum.

Books by James Grabill

Reverberation of the Genome (poems) Cyberwit, 2021

Eye of the Spiral (poems) UnCollected Press, 2021

Branches Shaken by Light (poems) Cyberwit, 2020

Sea-Level Nerve, Book Two (prose poems) Wordcraft of Oregon, 2015

Sea-Level Nerve, Book One (prose poems) Wordcraft of Oregon, 2014

October Wind (poems) Sage Hill Press, 2006

Finding the Top of the Sky (creative nonfiction with poems) Lost
       Horse Press, 2005

An Indigo Scent after Rain (poems) Lynx House Press, 2003

Lame Duck Eternity (wild poems) 26 Books chapbook, 2000

Listening to the Leaves Form (poems and prose poems) Lynx
       House Press, 1997

Through the Green Fire (creative nonfiction with poems) Holy
       Cow! Press, 1995

Poem Rising Out of the Earth and Standing Up in Someone (poems)
       Lynx House Press, 1994 (Oregon Book Award, 1995)

In the Coiled Light (poems) NRG chapbook, 1985

To Other Beings (poems) Lynx House Press, 1981

Clouds Blowing Away (poems) Seizure and kayak Press, 1976

One River (a reverie of poems) Momentum Press, 1975